The Water Cycle

written by Jon Adam
illustrated by Bob Dellinger

Contents

Harcourt

Orlando   Boston   Dallas   Chicago   San Diego

www.harcourtschool.com

The water you drink today was on Earth in the time of dinosaurs. This is because the same water changes all the time. These changes are called the water cycle.

2

As the sun heats the surface of bodies of water such as oceans, rivers, streams, and lakes, water evaporates. It changes into a gas called water vapor.

3

Water vapor rises with the warm air. As it rises, it cools and condenses. It changes back into drops of liquid water. The water drops join together to make clouds.

4

The water drops get bigger and heavier. When they get too heavy to stay up, they fall as rain.

If the air is very cold, water drops fall as snow, or flakes of ice. Sometimes they fall as sleet, or rain mixed with snow. They may also fall as small balls of ice called hail.

When rain falls on land, some of it is taken into the roots of plants. The plants pass water vapor out through their leaves into the air.

Most water that falls on land sinks into the ground. The water moves through the ground into lakes, streams, and rivers.

The water from lakes, rivers, and streams flows into oceans. Almost all of the water on Earth is in the oceans.

The sun heats the surface of oceans, lakes, streams, and rivers. The water cycle starts again, just as it did in the time of the dinosaurs. Just as it always will.

Glossary

evaporate Water evaporates, or changes into a gas, when it is heated.

water cycle The water cycle is the way water moves from the air to Earth and back again.

water vapor The gas that is formed when water evaporates is water vapor.

Index

Teacher/Family Member

Ask your child to dramatize the water cycle. Your child should take the part of a raindrop and explain how the raindrop changes as it goes through the cycle.

Science Vocabulary: *evaporate, sun, water cycle, water vapor*

Word Count: 242

Grade 2 Book 8   0-15-314871-3

Ordering Options   0-15-316218-X   Package of 5
                    0-15-316232-5   Earth Science Package, Books 5–8
                    0-15-316227-9   Grade 2 Package, Books 1–12

10   179   10 09 08 07 06 05 04 03 02

Science

Harcourt